Blue Peter

£2

BOOK
32

Written by
Anne Dixon,
Steve Hocking and
Richard Marson

This Blue **Peter** book
belongs to

Kirsty Nicholson.

Age eight

Blue Peter

Contents

HELLO THERE!

And welcome to the thirty-second Blue Peter book. It's packed full of our favourite highlights, but so much has happened since Book 31, it's been difficult to know what to include and what to leave out.

You can read all about our adventures in Vietnam, Japan and New Zealand. As usual, there are some great ideas to make and bake. Find out how your hard work has changed the lives of thousands of older people all over the UK. We hope you'll love the new photographs of little Meg who has grown so much. Not to be left out, Mabel and Lucy made Blue Peter history when they became the first-ever programme pets to travel to Europe with their new passports.

2001 was the first time that Blue Peter was on all year round – and in October we celebrated our 3500th programme with some of the top presenters from the 60s, 70s, 80s and 90s.

But, the most important event in the last twelve months was a very special visit to the Blue Peter studio by none other than Her Majesty the Queen. She was delighted to be presented with the programme's highest honour, a gold Blue Peter badge, and smiled when told it entitled her to free entry to the Tower of London!

We have had so much fun on the programme and some of the best ideas have come from you, so please keep on sending them and telling us what you'd like to see. We're all looking forward to hearing from you!

Rome Wasn't

O ne of the things we enjoy about making Blue Peter is the variety; one day interviewing Westlife or learning how to be a rally driver, the next dressing up and finding out what life was like hundreds – even thousands – of years ago!

When we decided to hold a grand Roman banquet in our studio, we had no idea just how much hard work it would be. Probably the biggest challenge was for our designer, Alison, whose job was to create an authentic-looking set that would bring ancient Rome back to life in twenty-first century West London.

Alison did loads of research using books and

the internet, before drawing up detailed plans for her team of carpenters and painters. In the end our triclinium, or dining room set, was too big to fit in our normal studio, so we had to take over the studio next door!

It was a big day for costume and make-up, too. Simon found his elegant toga surprisingly comfortable, if a bit draughty, and was impressed to learn that this was one of the reasons why the Romans invented underfloor heating. Konnie and Liz wore wigs, as Roman ladies favoured elaborate curly hair styles which took hours to create.

Everyone had Roman names. Simon became

Simonicus, Konnie, Konnila, and Liz, in her role as a grand guest, the haughty Lady Barkonius. No prizes for guessing who played the slave at the banquet. That job fell to Matt!

The most important thing at any banquet is the food, and putting on an impressive Roman spread took some doing. Luckily, many Roman dishes are still popular today – they even had a version of ice cream. Made without milk or cream, using crushed ice and fruit juice, it probably tasted more like sorbet.

P.S. Everything we couldn't eat we shared out among the Blue Peter production team. They hadn't eaten so well in weeks!

Built in a Day
(actually it only took a few hours!)

All in all, Lady Barkonius had a lovely time at Konnila and Simonicus's banquet. Even slave boy Matt wasn't left out. It was the custom for leftovers to be eaten by the slaves and, given the huge amount of food for just three people, Matt was in for a bit of a feast.

The Blue Peter website is one of the most popular CBBC sites because it's full of great features and things to do. It's also useful for the Blue Peter team because the message board keeps us in touch with your opinions – our school uniform poll on the website got us thinking about a subject that unites virtually every Blue Peter viewer...

Dressed

This, amazingly, is the current uniform at London's Hill House School. Simon thought the top half was quite cool, but he wasn't keen on the corduroy knickerbockers or the long socks! Eye-catching school uniforms are nothing new in this country, and the Hill House uniform wasn't the only unusual school attire we tried on.

Matt felt like a cross between a priest and a choirboy in this outfit worn by pupils at Christ's Hospital School.

The design dates back to the school's origins in Tudor times, and was given to poor boys when they joined Christ's to begin their education. Today the uniform is worn by boys and girls, and most of them say they like the fact that it is unique.

By the start of the twentieth century the Eton suit, named after the famous boarding school, had become popular. It may look like the smart suits you see at weddings, but it is everyday wear for pupils at Eton, including one of Britain's most famous schoolboys – Prince Harry.

Schoolgirls also had to wear uniforms, which often consisted of a tunic, a white shirt, a tie and a blazer. About 20 years ago it was still common for schoolboys up to the age of 13 to wear short trousers – hard on the knees in winter! While caps and hats were popular with schools, for most children they were just something else to lose, damage or get into trouble for!

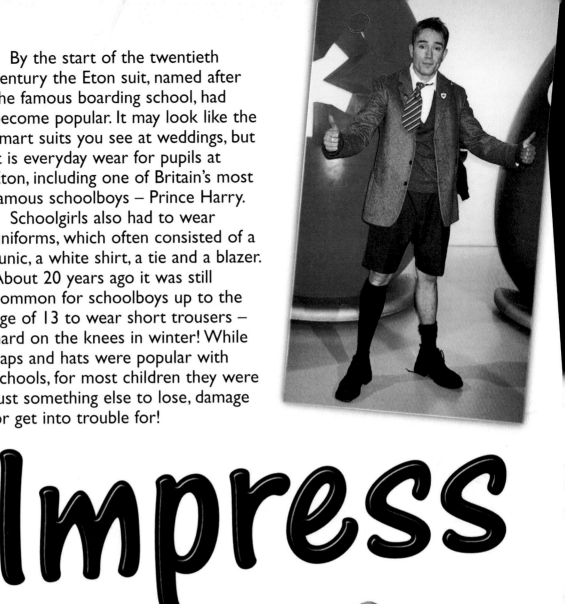

to Impress

In recent years, uniforms have become more comfortable and convenient. CBBC's very own school, Grange Hill, has had several changes of image, the most recent reflecting the fashion for fleeces rather than jumpers and blazers. But boys will still be boys – Simon, pay attention in class!

After we showed our potted history of school uniforms, we had loads of letters and e-mails. And the result of our school uniform poll? An overwhelming 75 per cent of you voted against them!

V ienna in Austria is one of Europe's most splendid cities. Liz will never forget the time she spent there with the world-famous Lippizaner horses.

On White

These horses are the stars of the Spanish Riding School, so-called because the horses originally came from Spain. The school's home is in the imposing Hofburg Palace in the heart of the city, and people come from all over the world to enjoy the shows held here.

The stadium is more like a palace ballroom, and it was a real treat for Liz to watch the horses 'dance' to the swirling music. They dance because they have been taught their unique movements. Liz was keen to find out more.

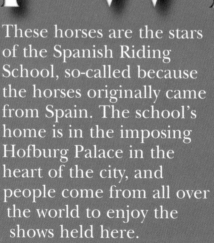

She was in luck because she had been invited to visit the little village of Piber where the Lippizaner horses are bred and trained. Piber is like somewhere out of a fairy tale, and the green fields around the school are full of horses and foals.

Liz was surprised to discover that the foals are born dark, becoming white as they grow older. By tradition there are no women riders at the school, so it was a great honour when she was told she could have a lesson on one of the famous white horses.

Horses

Liz is quite an experienced rider, but she was very nervous at first. Her instructor, Andreas, said her position on the horse was wrong, so she had to concentrate on getting the correct 'seat', as it is called, before he would allow her to move on from a simple trot and canter. The style of riding is called the High School, and is based on the natural walking movements of the horse.

At last Liz was allowed to try one of the 'dancing' movements. Andreas stressed that although he used a whip to control and direct the horses'

movements, it was only for the sound it made, never to hit them. Most of the horses have only ever had one rider during their time at the school, so the bond between horse and rider is very deep.

Although she wasn't wearing an immaculate uniform and performing in front of hundreds of tourists to the sound of one of Vienna's enchanting waltzes, Liz found it a strange and satisfying feeling to be riding high on a beautiful white dancing horse.

Adventures

The first thing that hit us when we arrived in Vietnam was the heat! And the roads, which were full of vehicles hooting their horns. In the capital, Hanoi, we tried the local breakfast, pho, and rode bicycles through the traffic, which wasn't as easy as it sounds as there didn't seem to be a highway code.

Liz met the national Takraw team. Takraw is a bit like volleyball but it's played with your feet as well as your hands. It's a tough sport.

Later in the trip we flew to Hué, a beautiful city. We filmed at an ancient temple to tell something of the history of the country. Matt dressed as an emperor and Konnie played two

in Vietnam

warrior-fighting sisters. People watching thought we were mad!

Meanwhile, Simon got soaked while sleeping in his hammock in the rainforest. He had a great time visiting a monkey sanctuary to see some of the important work being done to protect Vietnam's wildlife.

In Halong Bay, Matt met a fishing family, travelling with them on the boat that's also their home. It was pretty crowded! Matt helped land a catch of squid in the middle of the night.

Liz went off on an adventure of her own to visit the black Zao people, spending three days living in Ta Chai. It was a village with very few of the things that we take for granted in the UK. Liz said it really made her realize how lucky she is.

In Ho Chi Minh we met some children who spoke excellent English and were selling postcards to tourists to pay for their education.

We also met some Buddhist monks who invited us into their pagoda and put on a special ceremony while it poured with rain outside.

Another day we drove into the Mekong Delta. Can Tho is a riverside town with a floating market where you can buy almost anything. Konnie tried selling pineapples, while Simon helped Mrs Rose row her taxi. Konnie and Simon lent a hand with the rice harvest. It was hot and back-breaking work and after all their efforts, the rice they had harvested that day would be sold for just £22.70.

After fifteen eventful days, it was time to head home. We all felt we'd been away for a lot longer than two weeks, and over our last meal together we talked about Vietnam. Everyone agreed that it was a beautiful, fascinating country with incredibly friendly people.

It was an expedition we will never forget.

In Saigon, Konnie investigated the history of the Vietnam War, in which many thousands of people died. She filmed in the Cu Chi Tunnels. These were built by the Vietnamese Communist Army, and were so small that Konnie could only just fit inside them. Even so, soldiers lived in them for weeks at a time. Konnie met one of the fighters who had lost most of her friends in the war.

In November 2001 we launched our Wheel Help Appeal in aid of Help the Aged. It was a special cause that gave the Blue Peter team and viewers a chance to help thousands of elderly people, many of whom enjoy the show but are isolated and lonely.

WHEEL HELP APPEAL

Our target was to raise £500,000 to enable older people to get out and meet others. It's estimated that in Britain 29,000 senior citizens are lonely because they find it difficult to leave their homes. They can spend days or even weeks without speaking to another person. Minibuses and mobility scooters are the answer.

We wanted to help as many elderly people as possible to enjoy the sort of social life that children in the UK take for granted. We knew we couldn't solve the problem for everyone, but what we could do was offer help to groups like the older people Liz met in Dalmarnoch, Glasgow. Their minibus was old and couldn't carry wheelchair users, who often had to pay taxi fares to get to the local social club. If we could provide a new and specially-equipped bus, lots more senior citizens could get together regularly and enjoy each other's company.

£164·45p
Adam Bright + James Banfield

All over the UK as well as in Belgium, Spain and France, 25,588 viewers held Bring and Buy sales.

At the end of January we'd reached our target and Liz was able to drive the first minibus to Glasgow. It was a terrific excuse for a party and a very enthusiastic hokey-cokey!

A huge thank you to all the bringers and all the buyers who have really helped older people all over the UK to live more active and happy lives.

By summer 2002, thanks to you, we'd raised a million pounds – double our target!

Sweet like

Everyone in the Blue Peter studio knows that Liz is one serious chocoholic: "I just love it! Never mind once a day, more like three times a day!" But she admits that she's never given much thought as to where it actually comes from.

The main ingredient in chocolate is the cocoa bean, and although cocoa originally came from Central America, it's in Africa that two-thirds of the world's cocoa is now produced. Liz travelled to Odaho, a village in Ghana in West Africa. The climate in this part of Ghana is perfect for cocoa trees. The temperature is never above 30°C or below 15°C. What's more, it rains a lot, around 127 centimetres a year, which the trees thrive on. The farmers in Odaho all belong to a co-operative, which means that everybody gets paid a fair price for their cocoa. But, as Liz soon found out, it's hard work gathering the crop. She was there during the all-important harvest season, and because everything is still done by hand, she provided a welcome extra pair!

Chocolate

Liz helped farmer Mary Kurdyie to cut down the pods. When the pods were split open, she was surprised to see the beans inside. They are white and soft, and at this point they don't smell at all. The beans are left for several days to ferment under banana leaves. During this time, the beans begin to turn brown and the flavour just starts to come through.

Once they've dried out, the beans are packed into sacks to start their long journey from Africa to the countries where the chocolate is actually made. Belgium is very famous for its chocolate, and Blue Peter's other chocoholic, Konnie, went there to visit the largest processing plant in the world, on the outskirts of Brussels, the capital city. She was fascinated to discover how the beans from Ghana are treated in huge vats until they turn into liquid chocolate ready to mix and make into everything from bars and biscuits to sweets and Easter eggs.

To keep chocoholics around the world happy, the factory gets through 150,000 kilos of cocoa beans a day, much of it from Africa. Liz couldn't help thinking how strange it is that one of the most luxurious foods in the world is grown by farmers who have such tough lives, still harvesting their cocoa crops by hand.

STANDBY, GO!

That's the command used by the Royal Marines at the start of their famous assault course. After Matt had been put through his paces on the real thing, he and Konnie decided to build an assault course for action figures. Here are some ideas for making one of your own. You can make your course as tough as you like!

You will need:
2 sturdy, shallow cardboard boxes
    or one huge piece of cardboard
Scissors
3 empty one-litre juice
    cartons
A pencil or pen
Lolly sticks
Sticky tape
Card
PVA glue
Kitchen towel tubes
Gift wrap tubes
String
Plastic food trays
    (the sort that
    vegetables are
    sold in)
2 two-litre plastic
    milk bottles
2 fish finger boxes
    (or similar)
Brick-patterned
    wrapping paper
Paint and a brush
Papier-mâché
Pebbles
Foam pipe insulation
Action figures

Rope Regain

Climbing Wall

Tunnel

Build the assault course on two shallow cardboard boxes with one long side of each removed. Then, when you've finished playing, you can dismantle the course and stack it away. Or, if you have the space, you could use a huge piece of cardboard instead.

The Death Slide

1 To make the Death Slide tower, cut the top flaps off two juice cartons and tape the two open ends together.

2 Open up the top of the third carton and cut away the flap section with the pourer on it.

Draw and cut out a small square on one side just below the flaps. Make two more cuts on the sides of this carton and slide a lolly stick in between them. Fold and tape the remaining three flaps to create the top of the Death Slide tower. Tape this carton on top of the other two.

3 To make a base for the Death Slide tower, cut four pieces of card a little wider than the side of a carton and about twice as high as the width. Make sure the four pieces fit snugly around a carton before taping them together. Glue the base in a corner of one of the boxes. Stand the Death Slide tower in it.

4 To make the lower end of the Death Slide, first make the two post bases. Cut two 5.5 cm lengths from the wider of the two types of cardboard tube. Snip around one end of each and splay out the sections. Glue these roughly 6 cm apart in the corner diagonally opposite the tall tower. The two posts are made of 22 cm lengths of the narrower type of cardboard tube. Make slits for a lolly stick to slide between the tops of the posts, and push one through. Finally, tie a long piece of string between the lolly sticks at the top and bottom of the Death Slide.

Death Slide

The Tunnel

The Tunnel could be made from a plastic food tray and the two plastic milk bottles. Cut away two sides of the tray. Cut off the handle and base sections of the milk bottles. Fix the two milk bottle sections at right angles to each other in the tray and they will make perfect tunnels that could lead to a pebble-filled trench.

The Rope Regain

The Royal Marines use the Rope Regain to deliberately lose control of the rope, and then regain a hold to cross from one side to the other. Make one from a plastic food tray with goalposts at each end cut from cardboard tubes with string tied across the middle. Use four small sections of wider tube with the bottom edges splayed to form bases to attach the Rope Regain to the plastic tray.

The Climbing Wall

The Climbing Wall is a food box covered in brick-patterned paper (or you could paint the bricks yourself). The wall needs a base cut from another container taped to the assault course to hold it firmly in place.

Finally, make the assault course terrain with papier mâché. Build up the area around each piece of equipment to secure the bases. The tunnels need to be covered and camouflaged so be generous with the amount of papier mâché in this section. When the papier mâché is dry, paint the assault course in shades of brown and green.

The finishing touches are small pebbles in a trench between the tunnels, sections of foam pipe lagging cut up to look like tyres and a lolly stick fence.

We hope you enjoy making a unique assault course for your action figures. And have fun playing with it!

Meet Mabel

Mabel made a guest appearance on the programme in January 1996 as an RSPCA rescue dog. Everyone fell in love with the six-month old pup who had been found abandoned, starving and almost at death's door. She is now famous for her one blue and one brown eye and her floppy ear. Mabel is ball-crazy and loves long walks in Richmond Park. Her favourite food is roast chicken.

ROCK 'N' ROLL Christmas

I t's a bit of a tradition on Blue Peter that every Christmas we raid the BBC's dressing-up box, polish up our singing and dancing skills and put on a special show full of festive fun and frolics. The idea for our Rock 'n' Roll Christmas started when Matt wondered what Christmas was like in 1958, the year Blue Peter started.

In our version of 1958, things were not strictly accurate, but the story certainly gave Blue Peter viewers the chance to see us and a few of our closest friends as never before! The setting was Wood Lane High School. Matt was the new boy in school and, fresh from the country,

he hadn't heard of the rock 'n' roll craze. Super cool ST and his gang were less than welcoming, but luckily for Matt, dizzy Lizzie (who had a different hair-style every time we saw her) was quick to befriend him.

Lizzie's first bright idea was to get Matt a part-time job at the coolest hang-out in town, Hocking's Hotdog Hacienda. Here, Matt imagined taking his dream date, Konnie, to the high school hop. In fact, he was so busy day-dreaming that he spilled coffee all over her, so his prospects were not good!

At last Lizzie realized radical action was needed – and fast! She took Matt to the school gym where he was put through his paces and transformed from fool to cool just in time to unveil his super-smooth, brand-new image at the hop. Konnie was amazed.

Even ST became a mate when the new-look Matt turned hero to rescue ST from a pounding from his arch-rival, Big Richard.

The hop – and our show – ended with a song called 'We Go Together'. Packed with fantastic frocks, big song and dance numbers and a good old-fashioned happy ending, the team's rock 'n' roll Christmas had turned out to be a whole lot of fun!

ANE HIGH
MAS HOP
958

Meet George

George is a Mediterranean spur-thighed tortoise who joined the programme in 1982. He is around 50 years old, making him the oldest member of the team. He is nicknamed Speedy as he can race across the garden at a terrific pace. George loves the company of other tortoises and his favourite food is broccoli.

CHEERS!

Exotic fruit drinks are expensive to buy, but if you follow these delicious recipes you can make them for a fraction of the price. They're full of flavour as well as packed with goodness to boost your energy levels. Enjoy these drinks any time of the day.

Tropical Super-Booster

2 large or 3 small bananas, peeled and chopped
½ a small pineapple, peeled and chopped (or 4 pineapple rings canned in juice)
2 tablespoons of natural yoghurt
About 6 ice cubes

Place the bananas, pineapple, yoghurt and ice cubes in a blender. Switch on for about 20 seconds, or until you can see that everything is well and truly squished. Pour into glasses, decorate with fruit and umbrellas, and serve immediately.

Raspberry Super-Booster

250 ml fresh orange juice
100 g frozen raspberries (or fresh raspberries, blackberries or strawberries when in season)
I large banana, peeled and chopped

Allow the raspberries to thaw slightly, then pop them into a blender with the other ingredients and whizz for 20 to 30 seconds. Decorate the glasses with fruit if you wish. Then serve immediately (with ice cubes if you've used fresh fruit).

One Matt

eg may be nearly two years old, but she's still young enough to learn new tricks. As well as settling down as a member of the Blue Peter team, she is also training to be a fully-fledged sheep dog.

and his Meg

Border Collies are naturals when it comes to herding, and after breakfast, Matt and Meg head straight off for an early morning practice session with the small flock of sheep that live behind Matt's cottage.

No matter what the day has in store, Meg is Matt's priority. If it's an early call to the Blue Peter studio, it's an even earlier one in the field with Meg. She could keep going all day, but millions of viewers want to see her on TV so it's off to work for the pair of them. Meg loves nothing better than being strapped into her dog's seat belt, sitting up front in the car with Matt and watching the traffic go by as they travel to Television Centre to present Blue Peter.

During the day, Meg has several runs in the Blue Peter garden and enjoys rounding up a football which is also useful training! She loves a romp around the studio, too. Her favourite pal is Lucy, but any passing cameraman will do.

Everyone on the programme loves to play with Meg, and wherever Matt goes, Meg is sure to follow. She sits quietly while Matt does a sound recording, but when it comes to hearing the programme signature tune, Meg is bound to bark. She just loves being a part of the show. At the end of a long day, Matt and Meg head for home, but the day's not over until she's had another run before settling down to a good night's sleep.

By now she's so tired, she doesn't need to count sheep!

7.00

8.45

10.00

14.00

17.30

SUMO AND SUSHI

Twenty-six million people live in Tokyo. It's one of the busiest and most exciting cities in the world, and Konnie and Simon jumped at the chance to film there with the winners of our robot competition.

"We all loved it", says Konnie. "Japan has such a great mix of old traditions and the very latest gadgets. I especially loved the mobile phones. And I got to try out as a sumo wrestler, which isn't something that happens every day!"

Visitors have long been fascinated by Japan. For over 200 years it was isolated from the rest of the world by its military leaders, the Shoguns. Japan was seen then as a very interesting and mysterious place. Today, Tokyo is a world centre for business, but the traditions of Japan are still very strong. Simon found this out for himself when he joined actors recreating the lives of the Shoguns and their Samurai and Ninja followers.

Japan is also famous for its food and, in recent years, sushi -- raw fish and rice -- has become popular all over the world.

"I love food", says Simon, "but even I was a little nervous when I was told I'd be trying a type of sushi so dangerous it was banned by the Shogun!"

"Blowfish sushi is a real delicacy," says Konnie, "but parts of the fish are poisonous. It can only be prepared by special chefs but, even so, each year people die eating it! Apparently if you survive for 30 minutes after the meal you're OK. It was a long 30 minutes, I can tell you!"

"I really enjoyed Tokyo's hot springs," says Simon. "The region has earthquakes and volcanoes and the hot springs are put to good use. It's strange soaking in a public bath outdoors, but very relaxing. The oddest thing was having to wash before you bathe!"

"If that felt strange it was nothing compared to joining Tokugo Saito for a lesson in Sumo," says Konnie. "Everyone thinks of very large men when they think of sumo wrestlers." Tokugo Saito is one of a new generation of female sumo wrestlers who have taken up the sport in recent years as it seeks to be recognized by the organisers of the Olympics.

"She fitted me in a traditional Mawashi, a special pair of pants,' Konnie continues. "Then it was time to wrestle. I think that was one of the most unusual days in my time on Blue Peter!"

The last night was spent with our competition winners eating a farewell meal.

"It was sushi again," says Simon. "This time we were assured that there was nothing on the table that could kill us!"

Changing Blue Peter Rooms

BEFORE

We had just two days and £500 to get the job done.

Linda ordered the area to be stripped of furniture and photographs. These had been attached to the walls with nasty, black, sticky stuff that left a terrible mess. Then it was 'rollers at the ready' and the walls were transformed with two coats of cream emulsion.

Linda's idea was to make the walls look a bit like the sea so she'd brought stencils and two shades of blue paint. Linda asked Andy to transform our rectangular coffee table by making it a new top in the shape of the hull of the Blue Peter ship logo. Clever! He was also making tall shelf units so we could display the programme's souvenirs.

The chairs needed new covers, and Linda thought blue, grey and red would be just right. It's amazing what you can do with a staple gun and a piece of fabric! At the end of day one, everyone was exhausted, and worried that the job would not get done on time.

On Sunday morning, Konnie and Liz had started stencilling patterns on the walls long before Linda arrived. The room looked bigger and cleaner already. Then it was Andy's big moment. His tall shelf units looked excellent, as did the coat of red paint on the television cupboard and the matching table top above our mini-fridge.

Time marched on. Linda had bought ready-made curtains to hang in front of

On Blue Peter we often change the look of the show, but what we hadn't done since the programme started going out three times a week was to cheer up the 'soft seating area', the part of our office where we have meetings, watch the programme being transmitted, eat lunch... **It was long overdue for a make-over.**

Konnie and Liz thought they'd enlist the help of experts to transform the area over a weekend. So, step forward Changing Rooms' Linda Barker and Handy Andy!

the filing cupboards, so we screwed in curtain poles and hung the soft blue curtains from them. Then the furniture was put back and we added the accessories. Linda had cleverly scanned photographs of every single one of Blue Peter's 29 presenters and manipulated the images on her computer. They looked like Andy Warhol's pop art. The final touch was a lovely bunch of flowers, and on Monday morning, what did the team think?

Absolutely fabulous!
P.S. Thank you very much, Linda and Andy.

AFTER

It's no secret that Liz really loves clothes and keeps a close eye on all the latest looks. So when she was told that we were planning to fill the studio with a big fashion parade of funky new skirts by some of fashion's top designers, she was thrilled. "Can't wait to try them on," she told the producer. "Ah, but you won't be, I'm afraid," came the reply. "These are skirts for MEN!"

MEN IN SKIRTS

The skirts were the stars of a big new exhibition, and to model them to full effect we invited along a few of our male friends from CBBC. Not surprisingly, none of them had ever worn a skirt before. Some took a bit of persuading before taking to the catwalk and parading their new look in front of the Blue Peter cameras.

Simon and Matt, on the other hand, have worn skirts and kilts a few times over the years (no one will ever forget

their not-so-ugly sisters!) so are comparatively old hands when it comes to skirt-wearing. In fact Matt took quite a shine to his creation, a kilt with a twenty-first century twist. Called the 'utilikilt', it is made from cotton canvas and, with its plentiful pockets and useful clips for hanging tools, is perfect for electricians, painters and farmers!

Simon really stood out from the crowd in his groovy, green Oswald Boateng suit. It features a long, pleated skirt over trousers and Simon reckoned the vibrant colour was a clue to its purpose – to make other office workers green with envy!

We asked our leggy models if they thought skirts for men would catch on. Despite the fun they'd had casting off their trousers for the afternoon, the majority gave them the thumbs down. For one thing, the boys wondered how girls put up with all the draughts!

Liz watched from the sidelines and provided an expert commentary for our unusual fashion parade. However, when the item was over she jumped onto the catwalk and had just one thing to say to the boys, "Next time, I'm wearing the skirts around here, OK."

Ice Hotel

"Jukkasjarvi in Swedish Lapland is the furthest north I've ever been," says Matt. "It is 200 kilometres north of the Arctic Circle and very cold. At minus fifteen degrees it's the sort of town you need to wrap up warm in. After a day's filming you're really looking forward to a nice warm bed – so how come I'd travelled all that way to sleep on a block of ice?"

The 'ice hotel' where Matt stayed in Jukkasjarvi is famous. Everything is made of ice, from the walls to the windows, from the beds to the chairs and tables. It is rebuilt every October with 30,000 tonnes of snow and 4,000 tonnes of ice.

"It has 51 bedrooms and they're all freezing!" says Matt. "Still, the owner said the temperature in the rooms was only minus five degrees so it could have been worse." The hotel hosts weddings, babies are baptized in its ice church and

it even has its own ice cinema, though Matt didn't see any ice creams!

Making things from ice is catching and, as he'd travelled alone, Matt made himself an ice 'Meg'. There was no chance of her melting until springtime when the whole hotel starts to thaw.

"Sleeping was difficult," says Matt. "I'd been told not to wear too many clothes so that there was a good layer of air between me and my sleeping bag. That was fine but I just couldn't nod off. I don't know whether it was because my face was cold but I lay awake for hours. After a while I needed to use the toilet, and that was when wearing one layer of clothes didn't seem such a good idea!"

The crew were all sleeping in a nice warm cabin in the town. They'd left 'Meg' and Matt to freeze together at the ice hotel and they'd promised to wake him in the morning.

"I'd just got off to sleep when they came in!" Matt remembers. "It was a terrible night's sleep but I didn't mind. How many people can say they've slept in a room and on a bed both made completely of ice?"

Cool Christmas

Trees

If you want a Christmas tree with a difference, follow these instructions and you'll end up with something cool and stylish. And you can pack this tree away and bring it out year after year – how green is that? The colour scheme is entirely up to you. If you want a metallic finish, gold or silver enamel paint looks good.

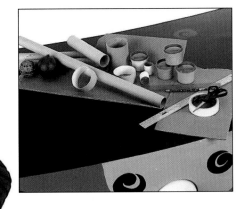

You will need:
Large cardboard boxes
Cardboard tubes of various sizes
Masking tape
Paper
All-purpose glue
Paint (acrylic, enamel, poster or
    tester pots of emulsion)
Christmas bauble
Ruler
Scissors
Pencil

1 Cut strips of corrugated cardboard from a box. All the strips should be 3.5 cm wide. Measure and cut three strips that are 78 cm long and make a bend on all three strips at roughly 22 cm. This section will form the base.

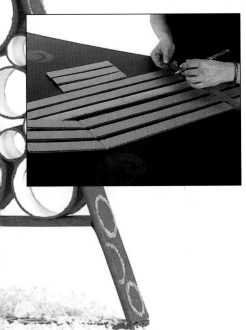

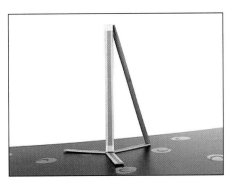

2 Stand the three strips together to form a triangle and wrap masking tape around the top and bottom to secure them in place. Cover the cut edges of the strips with masking tape or sticky paper. It has to be paper to ensure a good painting surface.

3 Measure the distance from the end of the base to the top of your tree, and cut three strips to this length. Attach them at the top and the base with masking tape.

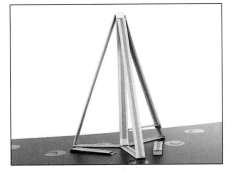

4 Cut three shorter strips that will become horizontals between the centre and the slanted strips. We cut ours 22 cm long. Score 2 cm at each end of the strips and peel back the top layer of paper so they can be glued in place.

5 Glue the horizontal strips a little way up from the base – roughly 6 cm – sticking the paper ends downwards onto the upright strips. When the glue has dried, you can paint the tree shape.

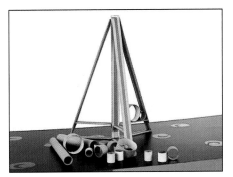

6 Cut the cardboard tubes into 3.5 cm wide pieces. Arrange them roughly in your structure. When you have cut enough to fill the tree, remove and paint them.

7 Paint the outsides of the tubes to match the tree but paint the insides in a variety of colours. Another variation is to paint the tree bright pink and inside the tubes white.

8 Put the tubes back in place, gluing where they touch the frame and each other. Top off your cool Christmas tree with a pretty bauble, glued into position.

Meet Meg

Meg was born on 6th December 2000 and is a black and white bundle of pure Border Collie mischief. She is already quite an accomplished sheep dog but loves nothing better than a good romp around the studio with her pal, Lucy.

Meet Kari

Kari and Oke are rescued moggies who came from the Wood Green Animal Shelter in September 1991. Viewers chose their names after the programme's summer expedition to Japan where karaoke was the new craze. Kari and Oke like a good tickle, especially from Simon and Liz.

Meet Oke

Blue Peter Beauty

Beauty is only skin deep, the saying goes. But, as we discovered, people have been pampering the body beautiful for thousands of years. Cosmetics date back to 4000 BC. Ancient Egyptians applied crushed black lead or 'kohl' to their eyes. The most famous beauty of the time was Queen Cleopatra. Her secret was to bathe in ass's milk to make her skin super-soft, a beauty treatment still used today.

In Elizabethan times only the rich could afford not to work in the open air, so looking pale was a sign of status. The palest of them all was Queen Elizabeth. Brushing egg white on her skin was one of her key beauty tips, but she wasn't too good at removing it. When she died, it was said she had inches of make-up caked on her face.

Liz tried a bizarre-looking facial machine which uses internal air cushions to put pressure on different parts of your face. It's meant to tone and relax the muscles, but Liz wasn't convinced. She thought the mask was claustrophobic and looked a bit scary.

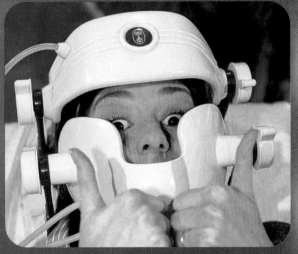

Natural ingredients are still big in beauty today. You can use cucumber on your eyes, have a mud face pack or use henna to dye your hair, but we wanted to try some of the brand new state-of-the-art treatments.

Matt gave top marks to the latest gadget from Japan – the Aqua Vibro. It looks a bit like a dishwasher but it's actually a high-tech hair-washing machine. As well as washing the hair, it massages the scalp using nozzles programmed to reach different parts of the head. It was very ticklish so Matt was soon in fits of laughter.

"Keep your hair on!" said Liz.

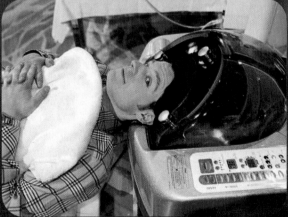

These 'flowtron boots' inflate round your legs and are supposed to improve circulation and stimulate your lymphatic system. Matt thought they made him look a bit like the bottom half of Mr Blobby!

IN AT THE L

The work of the Royal National Lifeboat Institution never stops. Whether you live by the sea or on a river, there is a RNLI boat that can be launched within minutes to answer an emergency call.

Lifeboat crews are trained to deal with emergencies, even those that could happen to them, like their boat overturning and everyone being tossed into the sea. Liz went to the Inshore Lifeboat Training Centre at East Cowes on the Isle of Wight to find out how they deal with that nightmare.

The capsize exercise took place on board an Atlantic 75, the same type of lifeboat as the Blue Peter lifeboats based at Beaumaris, Littlehampton and Portaferry. Instructor Scott Armiger and crew member Simon Cooper talked Liz through the drill before they tried it for real.

A crane was used to capsize the boat. Lifting straps were looped

EEP END

underneath so that just one side would be lifted up. Following the emergency drill, Liz made her way to the back of the boat, got her head down and held on to the emergency handle. The boat capsized very quickly. The rule is to stay in the boat until it has turned over. Liz found it very odd with the boat upside down on top of her, but she didn't panic as it was light, and the air pocket meant she could breathe. Liz scrambled for the whistle to give one big blow which told everyone that everything was OK.

The engines cut out and then it was time to get out from underneath the boat. Liz's dry suit helped to keep her afloat. She reached for the rope on the outside of the boat and, pushing on the emergency handle and pulling on the rope, she counted to three and bobbed up safely on the other side. Then, making her way to the stern, she gave the line on the transom a sharp tug and the boat automatically started to right itself.

The exercise had gone like clockwork. For Liz, it was an amazing experience, but for the RNLI crews, knowing this routine could be a question of life or death.

Good luck, and thank you to all of them.

BACK TO T

Simon and Matt are often asked what the toughest assignment is that they've tackled on Blue Peter. Both agree that it's the time they spent living in a recreated First World War trench.

They'd been invited to join the Khaki Chums, an unusual group of hands-on war historians who try to experience what it was actually like to live as a soldier in 1916, during a war in which millions of ordinary British men fought and died. The Chums use their expert knowledge to advise film and television productions, as well as raising money for charity.

Trenches were dug by both sides in the war along a front line which stretched for hundreds of miles across France. Men sometimes spent weeks at a time living in them. Although Simon and Matt were spared the fear of battle, death, and infestations of rats and lice, the trench they lived in was totally authentic. They soon found out what it was like to live and work in often thigh-deep, freezing, muddy water.

Everything the Khaki Chums use is completely realistic, from the itchy woollen uniforms (and badly fitting underwear) to the revolting food.

This was bread, tinned 'bully' beef and sweet tea made with condensed milk. They had to shave with First World War razors (Simon cut himself within seconds), clean their teeth with tooth powder (Matt said this was a bit like using talc) and spend long, boring hours on sentry duty.

Constant rain and biting winds didn't help. Just like the troops in the First World War, Simon and Matt got very little sleep in the trench. Their lowest point came in the early hours of the morning when it was pitch black and the only warmth came from a small fire.

What got them through was the support and friendship of the other lads – and even this was authentic. The Khaki Chums have spoken to surviving First World War veterans, all over 100 years old now, and many of them say that the soldiers fought, not for King and country, but for each other.

When their time in the trench came to an end, Simon and Matt weren't sorry. Their short experience had given them a glimpse of the feel, the taste and the smell of one of the worst wars in human history.

HE FRONT

DEAR Blue Peter

ere are just a few of the thousands of letters sent in each year by **Blue Peter** fans who write to tell us what they've made and the fun they've had doing it!

AHOY THERE!

We decided to make the Blue Peter logo from stones and pebbles we have in our garden. We think it looks GREAT! Blue Peter is our favourite programme because it has lots of good ideas for things to make.

Sophie and Rebecca Wilson and our friend, Ashleigh. All age 10. Newcastle-upon-Tyne

BROWNIES WITH LOVE

I made the chocolate brownies that you showed. They tasted really great! My brother and I made the Valentine card, too. That was for my mum because I love her. She always helps me with the Blue Peter makes. Thank you,

Sophia Singh. Age 7. Telford

KEEP YOUR PLACE

This is a photograph of me and the Blue Peter bookmarks. They were great fun to make. I use the Meg one every night when reading.

Cormac Long (your No 1 fan). Age 10. Middletown, Co Armagh

CHRISTMAS DECORATIONS

We made your Nativity Scene. Although it took some time, we did it. It was very good. My mum took some pictures on my camera. I love your programme.

Fritha and Iona Turner
Age 8 and 6.
East Malling, Kent

MAGICAL

We really enjoyed making the castle but it definitely took lots more than the 5 minutes you took on the programme.

From Toby Hind. Age 6. Leeds

PURRFECT...

We made the cat cosy for our kitten, Holly. She loves it as you can see! Thank you for the good idea.

Love from Katie Higson
Clitheroe

AWAY IN A MANGER

This picture shows the crib set we made. We had lots of fun making it.

From Geraint, Rhodri & Catrin Morris. Age 8, 6 and 4. Ross-on-Wye

EDIBLE CATHERINE WHEELS

I made some Bonfire Night Cookies. I love watching your programme.

From Lianne Toher
Briston, Norfolk

SLEEP TIGHT

After watching Konnie make the drawstring sleepover bags, me and my sister were inspired to make our own. We really enjoyed making them and we're really pleased with them

From Victoria Imrie. Age 12. Chester

WIZARD CASTLE

We followed your idea of making the Hogwarts™ castle out of cardboard boxes but we have added more things onto it. The first thing is a swivelling trap door on the base of
... it leads into a secret
... thing is a

Land of the Long White Cloud

The first people to settle in New Zealand were the Maoris, who called it Aoterea – the land of the long white cloud. Simon started his journey on Maori sacred land. The Maoris believed, and still believe, that everything in nature has a spirit and purpose.

"Before we could do any filming we needed to be welcomed by a warrior who would challenge me," says Simon. "My guide was Karleen, whose family are Paparoa Maori people. She'd taken me to a village where her family held their special ceremonies like weddings and funerals. There I was welcomed by Shannan, the warrior, who wasn't that scary. I had to stand very still and look him in the eye – oh! – and never turn my back on him. Mind you, one look at the size of the spear he was holding made sure I wasn't going to do that!"

Thirteen per cent of all New Zealanders are Maoris.

Their culture hasn't always been respected, and Karleen and Shannan are determined to preserve it for future generations.

Maori tradition is full of legends. One is that over a hundred years ago a group of tourists spotted a ghostly war canoe. Local people saw this as an omen, and eleven days later Mount Tarawera erupted, destroying the area.

SLOW DOWN!
PENGUINS CROSSING
KIA TUPATO!
HE KORORĀ E WHITI AN...

"I flew over the volcano and landed at the top," says Simon. "Then I ran all the way down into the crater. It was an awesome experience!"

New Zealand is a land of remarkable natural wonders with two main islands. On the North Island, Simon was invited to try white-water rafting on the Kaituno River, which is full of rapids. Simon negotiated his way past treacherous boulders and over a seven-metre waterfall.

"It was a white knuckle ride, quite literally, and totally exhilarating."

Simon was also in New Zealand to launch our competition to name the British entry for the Americas Cup Challenge.

He started his day with the British crew, not on water but in the gym for a training session. The highlight of the day came later when Simon and the team sailed out of Wellington harbour on their stunning yacht.

A few weeks later Blue Peter viewers came up with the perfect name for the British team's yacht – White Lightning.

Pasta Power

Planning a pasta party? Then look no further than this page for a fantastic fool-proof recipe that tastes delicious.

If you fancy creating four big bowls of steaming goodness, here's what you'll need:

1 courgette, cut into sticks
1 red pepper, deseeded and cut into sticks
1 sweet potato, diced
2 garlic cloves, finely chopped
3 tablespoons olive oil
salt and pepper
300 g dried pasta shells or penne
200 ml tub crème fraiche
2 teaspoons wholegrain mustard
100 g grated Cheddar cheese

Start by preheating the oven to 200°C or gas mark 6.

When you've chopped up the courgette, pepper, sweet potato and garlic, place them into a roasting tin. Drizzle the olive oil over the vegetables and use a wooden spoon to toss them around and ensure they are well coated. Sprinkle with salt and pepper and put in the oven to roast for 15–20 minutes until they start to brown.

Bring a large pan of salted water to the boil and carefully add the pasta. Let it cook for 10–12 minutes and then drain.

Pour the pasta on top of the roasted vegetables, add the crème fraiche and mustard and stir together. Sprinkle with the grated cheese and serve immediately. Simply delicious.

The great thing about this recipe is you can experiment with different vegetables – plum tomatoes, aubergine or butternut squash. Sausages cut into chunks are also a tasty ingredient but we're sure whatever you use, the finished result will be mouth-wateringly good.

MYSTERY
WORDSEARCH

Here's a challenge for you! How quickly can you identify the people and pets in the photos on this page and then find their names in this wordsearch?

```
T N U R S K A Q Q L U G M L Y
Z E V K H O C C Y C C N S J L
A Z I I Q L C T C C F X U E W
O H X N L S J L U G H M B U S
A V R Y N J P A L Y U A S I F
U L T I Q O M R Y S M T L V E
C M I V E W K J F U X U C P R
G M E M E C F X Q P F I S N S
K M A X M I T Q Z A G R P S F
V I Y O W N C Y Z M X E I X Y
K V F M O Y M W O K E M M O Z
R T C A T G I L I Y O W L I Z
Z W U T N G S L U N A X K R R
U H Z T P G E O R G E Q M B Q
S D R P F K H I K A R I J Y J
```

1

2

3

4

5

6

7

8

9

10

The Tale of Beatrix Potter

S ince *The Tale of Peter Rabbit* appeared a 100 years ago, Beatrix Potter's magical stories have been translated into dozens of languages and enjoyed by millions of people. But, as Liz discovered when she relived Beatrix's story, her books started quite by accident.

Helen Beatrix Potter was born in London in 1886. From an early age she loved art and nature. Together with her brother, Bertram, she spent hours painting flowers and animals, including rabbits that the children tamed themselves. Years later she said, "I do not remember a time when I did not try to invent pictures and make for myself a fairyland!"

Her family was wealthy and rather dull, and Beatrix was often lonely, surrounding herself with pets that she smuggled into her room.

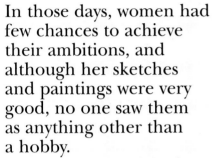

In those days, women had few chances to achieve their ambitions, and although her sketches and paintings were very good, no one saw them as anything other than a hobby.

Beatrix often visited the children of her old governess, and she told them stories about the pet mice and rabbits she brought with her. One day, when she was unable to visit, she sent a beautifully illustrated letter instead. It began, "I shall tell you a story about four little rabbits whose names were Flopsy, Mopsy, Cottontail and Peter."

It was this letter that Beatrix turned into her first book, *The Tale of Peter Rabbit*. At first no one wanted to publish it, put off by Beatrix's insistence that the book should be small enough for children to hold easily. So Beatrix used her savings to publish it herself. The 250 copies sold like hot cakes, and soon a company called Frederick Warne offered to publish 'the bunny book', as they called it.

This time it was printed in full colour. Within weeks, 8,000 copies had been sold.

The book's enormous success meant that suddenly, and quite unexpectedly, Beatrix Potter was in great demand. Luckily, she had plenty of ideas for more stories, all of them based on the animals, people and places around her.

The popularity of her 'little books' made Beatrix a rich woman. She used her wealth to buy thousands of acres of land in the Lake District countryside that she loved so much. She met and married a local solicitor, and so Beatrix Potter, the famous author, became Mrs William Heelis. She threw herself into running her farms and found she had less time and fewer ideas for new stories.

She lived in the Lake District until she died in 1943, leaving all her land to the National Trust so that it could be kept unspoilt and enjoyed by everyone. Beatrix Potter has given us two wonderful legacies – her enchanting stories and some of the most beautiful countryside in Britain.

59

Meet Lucy

Lucy was born on 14th September 1998 and in February 1999 she became the sixth dog to join Blue Peter. Her father is one of a long line of Golden Retriever show dogs. Lucy is as gentle as a lamb but can bark very loudly when excited.

Solutions

Our address is:
Blue Peter, BBC TV Centre London,
London W12 7RJ

Our home page is:
http://www.bbc.co.uk/cbbc
e-mail: bluepeter@bbc.co.uk

Written by Anne Dixon, Steve
Hocking and Richard Marson

Cool Christmas Trees and
Standby, Go! by
Gillian Shearing

Food by Phil Haynes

Photography by
Martyn Goddard, Richard Marson,
Chris Capstick, John Green,
Kez Margrie, Simon Thomas,
Alex Leger, Dermot Canterbury,
Adrian Homeshaw, Rob Franklin,
BBC Picture Publicity and
Blue Peter viewers

If we have left anyone out
we are sorry.
The authors would like to thank
the whole Blue Peter team for
their help and ideas.

Every effort has been made to
contact the copyright holders for
permission to reproduce material in
this book. If any material has been
included without permission please
contact the publisher.

First published in 2002 by
BBC Worldwide Limited
Woodlands, 80 Wood Lane,
London W12 0TT

Designed by Full Steam Ahead

CAPTIONS FOR PAGES 2–3

1 Simon and Matt joined the Royal Marines for a gruelling session of PE in the mud.

2 Mabel let fame go to her head – just check out those shades!

3 A studio full of famous faces – or the next best thing – as we met some celebrity lookalikes.

4 Gnome is where the heart is – we won't forget the day we were all turned into garden gnomes!

5 Matty G asking all Blue Peter viewers to show him a bit of "respec"!

6 We surprised pop star Sophie Ellis Bextor when she sang on the show by inviting back her mum – Blue Peter presenter number 13, Janet Ellis.

7 Take a chance on Matt – complete with blonde wig as one of the Swedish supergroup Abba.

8 Soaking up the sun on the Isle of Wight during one of our live outside broadcasts.

9 To celebrate St George's Day, the Royal Regiment of Fusiliers filled our studio with the sound of drumming.

10 Simon and Liz all dressed up in traditional Austrian lederhosen and dirndl.

PUZZLE ANSWERS

Page 57 Mystery Wordsearch

1 Lucy; 2 Liz; 3 Oke; 4 Simon;
5 Meg; 6 Konnie; 7 Kari; 8 Matt; 9 George;
10 Mabel.

THE BOYS FROM BLUE

When top boy band Blue first appeared on the programme, we themed the whole show on the colour blue in their honour! Since then, Lee, Duncan, Simon and Antony have been back several times, and as well as belting out their latest hits, they've also been stranded on our Fan-tasy Island. Fan-tasy Island is where Blue Peter viewers get the chance to meet their top idols, from movie stars and sports heroes to pop celebs.